T0129852

THEIR DAUGHTER,
MY BABY

Sometimes the greatest act of love is letting go…

MARIA SALAZAR SUGGETT

BALBOA.PRESS
A DIVISION OF HAY HOUSE

Balboa Press books may be ordered through booksellers or by contacting:

Balboa Press
A Division of Hay House
1663 Liberty Drive
Bloomington, IN 47403
www.balboapress.com
844-682-1282

Because of the dynamic nature of the Internet, any web addresses or links contained in this book may have changed since publication and may no longer be valid. The views expressed in this work are solely those of the author and do not necessarily reflect the views of the publisher, and the publisher hereby disclaims any responsibility for them.

The author of this book does not dispense medical advice or prescribe the use of any technique as a form of treatment for physical, emotional, or medical problems without the advice of a physician, either directly or indirectly. The intent of the author is only to offer information of a general nature to help you in your quest for emotional and spiritual well-being. In the event you use any of the information in this book for yourself, which is your constitutional right, the author and the publisher assume no responsibility for your actions.

Illustrations by Wylie Schwartz

Print information available on the last page.

ISBN: 979-8-7652-3268-2 (sc)
ISBN: 979-8-7652-3267-5 (e)

Library of Congress Control Number: 2022914476

Balboa Press rev. date: 08/09/2022

CONTENTS

PROLOGUE

I gave you up for adoption at birth.

1953

Saulimau Ioane Kalati

ONE OF THE NICEST MEN I have ever met in my lifetime, was a San Diego State University football player called Mau. He was the handsome, humble son of an immigrant family who was blessed with great athletic abilities. Your grandfather was a highly respected Samoan chief. I met them once at one of Mau's games and was touched by their kind smiles, a quality Mau also possessed. They didn't speak English, so while they didn't say much to me, I felt the warmth of their hearts, and that included great love for Mau. I felt included. Though Mau spoke perfect English, he was extremely shy and quiet – until he was on the football field. It was there his voice could be heard loud and clear. He earned a full scholarship to San Diego State University, a tremendous and well-deserved opportunity.

When your father was in high school, there was an article in the local newspaper about the family. They were so poor there was not always enough food to go around. Mau would often willingly sacrifice his meals so his younger sisters could eat, even though he himself needed the nutrition to play football.

II
1953

Maria Elena Salazar

I ALWAYS CONSIDERED MYSELF A NATURAL born mother, starting as a young child. Oldest of seven children - half Spanish, half German - I was born in Santa Fe, New Mexico. I assumed the typical Hispanic role of oldest daughter as #2 mom to my siblings. At 9 years old, with five children in our small bedroom, it was my job to diaper and give a bottle to my younger sister, even in the middle of the night, including on school nights.

I was the neighborhood babysitter, on weekends and throughout summer vacations. At 14, I stayed at our neighbor's home for two weeks, fully responsible for their 13-year-old daughter with Cerebral Palsy. She was much taller than me, but curled up in her bed and diapered, she was like a large infant. We were a larger than average family in those days, and vacations for us were mostly camping or day trips to theme parks, so I was available to babysit most of the time.

In high school I was a teacher's aide in a Cerebral Palsy unit in an elementary school, and after high school graduation worked at a residential home for special needs children. I worked in the "infant unit," made up of any size child or teenager that wore diapers.

I felt motherhood was my natural role in life, something I couldn't wait to become. I was blessed with two parents whose focus in life was family. Both hard workers and great partners in both love and life, they put my siblings and me through prestigious private schools, and we lived in a very structured environment built on the foundation of family. We said our prayers every night on our knees, all lined up in our family room with our father watching and listening. We asked for blessings for our family, then kissed our parents goodnight. We spent many wonderful times with relatives, and camping was our mode of family vacations. We couldn't afford hotels or even restaurants, but we had a blessed life. While our home life was very structured, it was always planted firmly in our minds that family came first – above all else.

Sadly, two of my sisters died very young. Michaela was a stillborn 11 months after I was born, buried in New Mexico. Consuelo Lucia "Shoo Shoo" was born when I was 13. She died of crib death at 15 months old. Shoo Shoo was my responsibility to bathe and put to bed each night, and I was the last one to be with her before she died. I always wondered if I had done anything wrong that night. No one mentioned anything. I packed my feelings away (to be brought out many times over the years), and life went on. Her death and my role (right or wrong) haunted me for decades.

When my mother was in her final days, 50 years later, I asked her a question I had always wondered about.

"Was it my fault that Shoo Shoo died?" I asked.

"Why would you ask me that?" She asked me.

"Because no one told me it was, and no one told me it wasn't," I replied.

"It was absolutely not your fault." She said.

And that was that. Things of both minor and major importance were not discussed in our family beyond daily responsibilities. A missed opportunity to heal hearts and souls.

III
1974

Your Conception

$\mathcal{I}$ MET MAU AT A HALLOWEEN party when we were both 21 years old at the home I shared with my roommates, and he was so tall, dark and handsome. His shy smile that extended to his warm eyes immediately drew me in. He was the friend of my roommate's boyfriend Mase, also Samoan. I was instantly smitten, and the feeling was mutual.

We easily fell into a relationship. It was great – our lives and friends merged comfortably and easily. Volleyball, beach parties, baseball games, and doing "the bump" at parties was fun and light-hearted. We never argued - we got along really well. I loved going to watch Mau play at the SDSU football games, with a big group of friends.

After about 5 months of dating, we became pregnant. As lame as it sounds, we were both surprised. Neither of us had had much sexual experience. He was very shy and I was raised in a very strict home. In today's world, 21 is not that young to accidentally get pregnant, but then it was. Then, you didn't hear much about young women getting pregnant, at least I didn't.

While we had a wonderful and caring relationship, we had not dated long enough to establish a future together. He was on a football scholarship at San Diego State. He worked part time for a moving company, living with roommates, while I was working at a small loan company, and not earning much, although I was very responsible. I started working there at 19, started saving money and getting credit established. I was living with two friends who I loved. I had a very nice life, and I was happy.

Although we were initially excited about my pregnancy, because of our feelings towards each other, we were not prepared to commit to marriage and a family. We discussed possible scenarios to figure out what to do. When I told Mau I didn't think we were ready for a baby, he told me that his family wanted to raise you, but they were living in a room connected to their church, and though his family was kind and loving, I wanted more for you. Maybe my very different background and upbringing from Mau's formed my opinions. By this time my parents owned a successful chain of restaurants in San Diego. Both of my parents were self-made. They both came from poor backgrounds, went to college, worked hard for opportunities, and were successful. But to be perfectly honest, while I wanted more for you, I wanted more for Mau too. This was his opportunity to make a great life for himself. I urged him to take full advantage of his football scholarship.

Whether it was the 1970's or my extremely sheltered and strict upbringing, there was not one divorced couple, nor one single parent in our circle of friends or family. There were no role models at that time to learn from. In essence, as much as I wanted to be a mother, I didn't have any idea how to raise a child responsibly on my own. And no other options seemed feasible. So, not knowing what else to do, I made an appointment for an abortion. The night before my appointment, I was watching TV, staring blankly at the screen. I just knew in my heart I couldn't go through with it. I cancelled the abortion first thing the next morning.

It must be said that I had short-lived fantasies of you, my unborn child, and me in an "us against the world" scenario. It was a grand adventure to be sure, but parenthood is more than an adventure. It soon dawned on me that the reality was I had no idea how to be a responsible parent, especially on my own. I just couldn't see how this could work. So, I decided to give you up for adoption. As soon as I made my decision, a sense of peace washed over me, and I never changed my mind.

First, I told my mother the news about my pregnancy and my plan to give you up for adoption. My mother accepted the news calmly and was very understanding and pragmatic about what I should do next. She said "Move closer to our house and we will take care of you."

The very next day I saw my father in the car next to me near our family home. I honked and waved. He saw me and turned his head away. I honked again and he would not look at me. It was then I realized that he was very upset with my situation, even though I told my mother that my plan was to give my baby up for adoption to "make things right." I called my mother who informed me I was disowned from my family and was not allowed to see my younger siblings. It was then that the seed of shame was planted in my mind and heart, to be watered and nourished by more shame and guilt over the years.

Again, in my mother's last days, she expressed a regret that she harbored for each of her children. The regret she held for me was that she didn't allow me to return home after I was disowned for being pregnant. She said, "You begged me to let you come home over and over, and I wouldn't let you. I regret that."

Immediately thereafter, other areas of my life toppled one by one in quick succession, like dominoes. I told my boss's wife I was pregnant. We were great friends outside of work. I often babysat their toddler. She held my hand and said "Don't worry, I'm your best friend, we will take care of you." The very next day, I was fired from my job by my boss for being pregnant and unmarried. I was shocked.

As my mother had suggested, I moved closer to my parents, away from wonderful roommates I had lived with for two years. Because I was not allowed to see my family, I spent most of this time alone. I recall many nights, crying, holding my teddy bear, a Christmas gift from my parents at age 16, like the lost little girl I was.

Your father was very upset about my decision because he wanted his family to keep you. We argued about it, going back and forth, but in the end broke up.

Ending our relationship was hard, but my resolve to right my "wrong" did not waver. I felt strong in my decision and yet was lost, lonely and confused by the abandonment by family and friends who had promised to help me. It was an extremely difficult time. Shreds of these feelings still show up when I feel abandoned, even decades later. But, true to my decision, I stayed healthy for you, determined to give you all I could that was within my power for as long as you were inside me. I went to a free clinic to get medical care, although my doctor was extremely kind and the care very good.

I resorted to going on welfare to survive financially until you were born. It was humiliating after my short tenure in finance, and the small financial gains I had made there. Ironically, I spent the last 15 years of my career teaching financial literacy across the country.

It bears asking - while the two women central in my life were supportive and understanding of my situation, were they overruled by the men in their lives? Was it because it was the early 1970's - a generation that was male dominated? Did I unwittingly bring shame to the two men I was counting on for unconditional love, but perhaps were unable to? Would it have been different had I been supported by my family, kept my job, and allowed to return home with my family? I would have stood by my decision to give you up for a better life, but it might have saved me from decades of shame that has affected me emotionally, even today. It could have gone much differently. But at that time, in that era, a solid, feasible alternative didn't seem to exist for me.

The social worker who facilitated the adoption was wonderful and nurturing. She informed me that she had found an affluent Mormon family with teenagers who wanted a child for whom they could offer a great life. It sounded like exactly what I wanted for you – a family that could give you and be everything I couldn't.

When I signed the adoption papers, I briefly saw your adopting family's name and address and wrote it down afterwards. Somehow it comforted me to have a sense of where you were going to be living, which was locally in San Diego. I never went to see where you lived; I just wanted to know where you would be. Not knowing where you were would have haunted me terribly.

IV
1975

Your Birth

WHEN YOU WERE BORN, I was put under general anesthesia near the end of my labor, and I never saw you. Mercifully, I was placed in a hospital room away from the maternity ward after you were delivered. Your adoptive parents picked you up from the hospital. I was happy to hear I had given birth to a healthy 7-pound 13-ounce baby girl. I went home empty handed and sad for me, but happy for you and your family.

My family accepted me back into the fold

shortly thereafter. The pregnancy and birth were never mentioned again. I felt so much shame in my heart. Life just went on. I started my life all over. I told no one for fear of being judged, shamed, or abandoned. I missed you every day. My biggest – and only - comfort was knowing that you were nearby.

I started dating a man I met at the same Halloween party where I met Mau. David and I started dating when I was five months pregnant. A handsome, popular, charismatic rugby player, he was 27 and had a son from his previous marriage that ended in divorce. He was the only person that truly showed up for me.

We were at a party once and I overheard a beautiful girl ask him, "She's pregnant with someone else's baby, why are you with her?"

"I love her," was his immediate reply. 48 years later, after a marriage that ended in divorce and two more children later, we are still friends, and he has never stopped showing up for me.

V
1976

*Your Adoptive
Mother Lorraine*

REBUILDING MY LIFE, I STARTED working at a local utility company. When you were an infant, I received a note card from your mother with a photo of you in a beautiful white dress. There was a waiting period of a year for the adoption to be irreversible and I had agreed to that, but your mother was kind and wanted me to know you were safe, happy, and loved.

After the adoption was finalized, I received

a letter from the social worker telling me our adoption case was the best she had ever seen in her career. To this day, I have the letter in my pink "Janet" folder, worn and soft from being read so many times.

VI
1978

Mutual Friends

$\mathcal{A}$T THE UTILITY COMPANY WHERE I now worked, our department hired a young secretary, Juli. She was a practicing Mormon in a nearby congregation, in the same geographic area you were living. We became instant friends, a friendship that continues to this day. Once I found out you possibly knew each other, and with my heart beating out of my chest, I "nonchalantly" asked her if she knew your family, and that I thought they had adopted a baby girl. Not knowing my reason for asking (sorry, Juli), she shared all she knew about you.

"The day Janet was born, Mr. Borg stood in front of the entire congregation and talked about how happy they were to have adopted her and how much they loved her."

Juli also remarked that, "She is an adorable, chatty little toddler who stands on the pews at church and talks to everyone around her."

Just hearing these small tidbits about you made my heart sing with joy. It filled my heart with warmth and happiness and affirmed that I had made the right decision for you.

VII
1980

Meeting Your Parents

MY FRIEND JULI WAS MARRIED in 1980 to a fellow Mormon and I was invited. I was excited and anxious, wondering if you or your parents would be there. At the reception, on the dance floor, a couple next to me were smiling kindly at me. Sure enough, they were your parents. They smiled at me and handed me a photo of 5-year-old you.

Your mother said, "She looks just like you and we see a lot of your personality in you." The swell in my heart was only dwarfed by my smile. I never saw them again, but I will never forget that day.

Many years of correspondence with your parents continued; cards, letters, and photos, all thanking me for the gift of you. My letters to them thanked them for their kindness and healing my heart. It was as if they knew exactly what I needed. Seems we were both blessed by your parents.

Years passed quickly. I now had two more children and a stepson from my marriage to David, but I kept track of how old you were. I was concerned that I would lose touch with you after you graduated from high school, not knowing your plans for college or if you would be married and leave the area. You were never far from my mind and thoughts.

VIII
1993

Meeting You and You
Meeting Your Father

SADLY, AND SOMETHING THAT HAUNTS me, is that your life has been punctuated by a series of losses. It leaves me wondering sometimes "what if" I had made different choices. Your sweet, kind adoptive mother Lorraine died of Alzheimer's when you were 18, after years of not being able to speak. You went to live with a wonderful neighbor family who adored you.

Also, when you were 18, just out of high

school, your biological aunt Mary called me to tell me that her brother, your father Mau, was dying of cancer and had three weeks to live. His most fervent wish was to see you, his only child, before he died. She asked me if I could make that happen. I promised her that I would make it happen, though I didn't know how.

I had by now begun my career in education in 1990. Miraculously, through a teaching colleague connection who I knew was Mormon in your ward, I was able to quickly get in touch with you with one phone call and we made a date to drive to Los Angeles from San Diego the following day to see Mau.

I showed up at your house, took a deep breath, scared to pieces about how this would go, knocked on the door, and out you came – a tall, beautiful young lady, with a smile that could light up the world, a glorious mane of dark curls, and your best friend for moral support. I was so happy to finally see you. The three of us chatted easily on the two-hour drive up and back, as if we had known each other forever, even though we had just met. The radio in my car was broken, but it didn't matter, there were no gaps in the conversation to fill.

Imagine how this day went - seeing Mau and his parents for the first time since I had dated him almost 20 years prior. Yet now, 19 years later, we were all together in Mau's hospital room! And most of all, we were all meeting YOU!!

Neither Mau nor his parents showed me any animosity for my unilateral decision to give you up for adoption. They smiled at me with the same warmth as the first time we met. And while your grandparents still did not speak much English, their love for you needed no words. At 5'8", you sat on your grandmother's lap with her loving arms wrapped around you. It was as if she didn't want to let you go. You sat on the side of Mau's hospital bed and talked easily and comfortably with him. I presented him with all the photos I had received through the years to fill him in on your life.

When we arrived back to your house that night, I didn't want the day to end, especially now that I had met you. You asked me if I wanted to see your bedroom. Of course, I said yes. I was amazed by how similar we were – a very clean, tidy room with many photos on the wall, something I have always decorated my homes with.

More than anything, I was in awe of the

poised, gracious young lady that you became. You handled the day with a grace that could only be the result of being raised with deep love, respect, and compassion for others. You made everyone feel special.

I still recall that day with wonder. What could have been a very difficult day, all things considered, it was a beautiful day. So much love in the room for each other despite the different paths that were taken.

Miraculously, Mau survived his illness.

IX
2003

Mau's Death

AFTER MEETING EACH OTHER, YOU and Mau began a great relationship that lasted ten years, until Mau's cancer returned and he passed away, just shy of turning 50. Although I had no role or responsibility in his life, I have always felt guilty that he never had more children, as I went on to have four more.

Your adoptive father died in 2015 — he and I stayed in touch for many years through written communication. He never stopped thanking me for the gift of you, and I never stopped thanking him for his cards and letters that very possibly kept my heart emotionally afloat when it came to you.

X
1997

Your First Marriage

YOU MARRIED A WONDERFUL, HANDSOME man named Mike. Unable to bear children of your own, you became foster parents for many infants and young children, and ultimately adopted three beautiful boys. Sadly, Mike passed away at 38 from cancer in 2013, leaving you a young widow and mother. You and I were now communicating by email throughout Mike's illness and passing. I felt blessed and honored to be a part of your life, albeit at a distance.

Isn't life curious sometimes? You were adopted and decided to become a foster parent and adopt children yourself. Would that have happened if your life had been different from the beginning?

XI
2014

Finding You on Facebook

YOU WERE A YOUNG WIDOW with three boys to raise. We communicated infrequently by email but stayed in touch. Whatever contact we had I was grateful for. At dinner one night, a dear friend asked me if it was true that our first child is our favorite. He was shocked when I suddenly burst into tears. My first child I gave up for adoption, I said, so I don't know how to answer you. That night, as soon as I returned home from dinner, I found you on Facebook. You accepted my friend request. And now there was another way to be in your life, which remains today.

XII
2015

Christmas Gifts

ℱOR CHRISTMAS THAT YEAR, YOU sent me a box filled with your favorite essentials – your daily must haves. Your four-page letter explained it was your way of helping me get to know you better. Gum, hand lotion, pens, note pads, car air fresheners — all sorts of daily items that gave me a close-up look at you in a fun and creative way. It was a brilliant way to bridge years of not knowing each other. Of course, I have your letter in my pink Janet folder.

XIII
2016

Seeing You Again

As OUR FACEBOOK CONNECTION CONTINUED, we agreed to meet in Utah one summer, as I was traveling in the area, and wanted to see you if possible. I had not seen you since you were 18 and it had been 20 years. Driving up to the restaurant I was overcome with emotion, sobbing, but of course you were your usual gracious self and made me feel comfortable immediately. Your three boys were adorable and sweet to me. I asked you how you were introducing me to the boys.

You said without skipping a beat, "I told them you're my birth mother." We had a lovely meal complete with lively, friendly conversation and big smiles. We took photos with the boys. I left fulfilled and grateful that the merciful adoption gods had blessed me once again.

Telling the world about you on Facebook was risky – based on my experience of abandonment I wasn't sure how the news would be accepted. After all, this was my "deep dark" secret known to few. I took a chance, bared my heart, and spoke my truth. I told my story to the world. To my surprise, hundreds of people not only loved the post, but many people also shared their own personal experiences with adoption in their family. The healing that had begun by your connection with me was now a full-fledged heart opening that released decades of shame. Light was shining in the place that had held darkness for so long.

XIV
2017

Your Marriage to Jacob

YOU REMARRIED A WONDERFUL WIDOWER with five children, and now have a blended family - eight children between you. That same year my parents passed away six months apart. Once everything was settled with my family, I decided to move to be near you. I saw this as my chance to have a closer relationship with you.

XV
2018

Living Near You

YOU AND YOUR NEW HUSBAND Jacob accepted me as a member of your family with open arms. Movie afternoons with the children, holidays together, visits to each other's homes - all ways of getting to know each other. I knew it was going to be a process and I was eager for more. One by one, your blended group of children started calling me Grandma and it still gives me a thrill. They each treat me with respect, and I love them dearly.

Over time, I relaxed more around you. At first, I was so nervous, not wanting to say or do the wrong thing and damaging a fragile, new form of our relationship. We had open and honest conversations about your adoption. I needed for you to understand how difficult it had been to let you go. Having been a foster and adoptive parent you said you understood completely. You said you had been raised by a wonderful family, you had older siblings that you were close to, and thanked me for my decision.

I had been desperately needing acceptance, validation, and forgiveness, perhaps more from myself than anyone else. I carried the burden of shame in my heart for decades. Without knowing it, once you "forgave" me, absolved me of wrongdoing, my heart began to heal. You brought light into the dark places in my heart where guilt, sadness and shame had dwelled for so long. You understood, and I needed that more than anything, probably more than I realized.

XVI
2019

Love From Afar Revealed

ONE DAY, I GAVE A folder of all my correspondence with your parents over the years, my pink "Janet" folder, to your husband Jacob. I said, jokingly, "This will show Janet how much I have always loved her, and I have been following ("stalking") her for her entire life, and that I have always loved her." I wanted you to see it. He did as I asked.

The very next day, you asked me if I would consider staying with your children for a week while you and Jacob traveled. You were opening your heart and home to me, allowing me to be a real part of the family.

To this day, we plan my visits around your travel with Jacob, and I get to stay with the children and see you when you return home. It couldn't be more perfect.

EPILOGUE

Sitting in the living room of your beautiful house, ready to fly home after one of several wonderful stays, I look up and see a piece of art from my parents' collection on a shelf. I gave it to you before I moved back to San Diego. It is a beautiful statue of a mother holding a baby in her arms. I especially wanted you to have that piece, as it reflected my long-held dreams of holding you in my arms. In that moment, I am overwhelmed with a feeling of awe and gratitude for my relationship with you and your family. Never in a million years would I have believed this was possible.

I shout up the stairs "picture time!" and eight beautiful children, none of whom contain a drop of my blood, come bounding out the front door for a series of photos with Grandma.

I never dreamed that we would someday be a part of each other's lives, but I suppose that's because I felt the relationship was one-sided; me wanting it. I didn't realize that you were open to knowing me also. I never take this gift for granted.

My pink "Janet" folder continues to grow with more photos of you and your family, cards and letters from you and your children.

You are Bob and Lorraine's daughter, and by the grace of God, my daughter as well. You are and continue to be a gift to those who are blessed to know you, and most of all, to me.

ACKNOWLEDGEMENTS

This book has lived in my mind for many, many years, each memory indelibly etched in my heart. While there are gaps in the timeline due to infrequent communication at times, there are no gaps in love.

Thank you first and foremost to Janet, for allowing me to share our love story.

To Connie Terwilliger, Norma Cazares, and Dan Sackheim for their eagle eyes and editing favors they bestowed on me.

To all my wonderful friends who read my several iterations, Linda, Margaret, Gloria, Irma, Jessamine, and Kelly, thank you.

To Kathy Floyd, my constant cheerleader.

Wylie Schwartz, you brought my dreams to life with your stunning and evocative illustrations.

Christopher Donach, you have stood by me for years with your design magic.

To my parents, you taught me to always do the right thing, no matter what. For that I am grateful. I only wish you had met your beautiful granddaughter. You would have loved her.

Printed in the United States
by Baker & Taylor Publisher Services